Fate of a Mullet

Poems by Mackenzie Thorn

Kansas City   Missouri

Spartan Press
Kansas City, MO
spartanpress.com

Copyright © Mackenzie Thorn, 2019
First Edition1 3 5 7 9 10 8 6 4 2
ISBN: 978-1-950380-80-0
LCCN: 2019956512

Design, edits and layout: Jason Ryberg
Author photo: Madison Thorn
All rights reserved. No part of this publication may be reproduced or transmitted in any form or by any means, electronic or mechanical, including photocopying, recording or by info retrieval system, without prior written permission from the author.

The author would like to thank the editors of these publications
where some of the poems in this collection first appeared
(in some form or another):

Bad Jacket and *Rye Whiskey Review*

TABLE OF CONTENTS

Food for Thought / 1

It's Best Not to Talk About It / 2

Coffee County Premonitions / 3

Pack Rats and File Cabinets / 4

Do It for the Money / 5

Hampton Ballerina / 6

Thrift Store Bride / 7

History Channel / 9

The Gates of Hell Don't Have a Doorbell / 10

314 Fallujah / 11

She Came in Through the Bathroom Window / 12

Moving Day / 13

Icarus / 16

Manifest Destiny / 17

Existentialism Is for the Rich / 18

Ramen Noodle Zombies / 19

Leap of Faith / 21

Elephant in the Tomb / 22

Bass Ackwards / 23

Realm of Hungry Ghosts / 24

The Black Hole / 25

My Frankenstein / 26

I Don't Take Care of My Things / 27

The Beats / 29

5 AM / 30

Giant Steps / 31

Linoleum Dreams / 33

I Thought We Was Kin? / 34

Barstool Brag / 35

Corner Store Mass / 36

Blood on the Maple Leaf / 38

Starry-Eyed Strays / 39

Silence / 41

Country Mouse / 42

Ultra Violet / 44

Whiskey Throttle / 46

The Nest / 47

Dick Cheney Shot Someone and
 Got Away With It / 48

I Love Lamp / 49

Fate of a Mullet

nihilism as it is experienced – the actual 'existential' sense of the meaningless and futility of life – is not the product of an intellectual theory...

-Viktor Frankl

Food for Thought

Written across the heavy yoke in which we carry
Scratched into the wood by fingernail
A hungry mouth fed with lead
Inevitably
Will be heard
Through voice of tongue
Or by gun.

It's Best Not to Talk About It

I should get sober and do yoga
Said Cat frankly to her reflection in the window

You should talk to someone
    said the Hound
His jowls rippling with concern

Maybe you're right...
Replied Cat.

Realizing it was their stop,
Cat pulled the chord and walked to the front of the bus.
The Hound opened his umbrella as they stepped out onto
    the sidewalk and offers Cat some shelter from the rain.
She smiles at his nature.
Relieved the Hound doesn't press the issue.
Cat snakes her arm around his as they begin the long
    silent walk home.
Their minds drift far from the rain,
And the busy streets,
And from each other.

Coffee County Premonitions

Smokestack lighting parades welcomed us at the gates of promised decadence
A sanctuary made holy by the boxed blood of Christ
Lost in the wine-stained routine chaos aside unwashed compatriots
Proudly slouching shoulders and bobbing heads like dead refugees in the Mediterranean
Listening close for the call of Gabriel's trumpet
Premonitions of hell fire picked at our brains like buzzards as we circled the burning barn
We waited until nightfall to wash ourselves in the sweet Cherokee spring
And begin the ghost dance to celebrate our neglect of fate
But behind the smiles and bloodshot eyes
The laughter and trembling skin
The pines and mud and Tennessee sun
We knew
This too must end
Like the sleeping cicada awakened by the chorus of spring
We too shall be released from our quiet cradles
And reclaim the coffee county valley once again

Pack Rats and File Cabinets

My grandmother rests in a white box,
Next to my first dog.
A coffin is too expensive,
Spanish is too romantic,
German is too exact,
And English is too plain.
There's no rush for a small box,
I would pay five thousand dollars for someone to move
    this coffee table though;
I would pay another thousand for my mother to be a mother.
I would pay,
I will pay,
For a peaceful sleep.
Another rib cage for my heart to keep safe.
Another shield and axe,
To be brave behind,
Another forgotten name to be inside.

I will hide behind
The sounds
Of my howls offered to the wind
Spread out like sin.
I need a fin to begin again.

Do It for the Money

Five thousand dollars were found in the parking lot.

Tucked away into a duffel bag
Wrapped together neatly with rubber bands.

They stood there, encircling their prize,
As the assumed civilized pale freaks they were,
Snickering with nervous fervor and sharing half-baked
    smiles at one another.
Trying to pretend,
Like they wouldn't murder each other for that money,
Like they had manners
Or called their mother.

As they chattered and boasted over dead horses.
I had my eyes on the scissors
    and waited for the first pale freak
        to make their last move.

The Hampton Ballerina

The crosswalk counts her in
He dives across the stage
Bounding under the full moon spotlight
Graceful as the light bugs
Fearless and free
Adorned by bouquets of trash
Cars bleep bravos
The audience patiently consumes the aesthetics
Before the streetlight turns green.
Her heart snapped at the reigns
But he was betrayed by her mind
Sliced his lover asunder
With a katana sword
Because he presumed herself to be God
Now she performs in an 8×10 stage
With iron bars as curtains
Never knowing for certain
What happened

Thrift Store Bride

I went to the thrift store hoping to find a winter coat.
I entered through the sliding doors and peeled around
the cash registers. Sweeping the floor with determined
strides towards the far last register. Once there, I can
make a left towards the coat section in the back of
the store. My head is angled towards the ground while
using the occasional glance to periscope my relative
distance to my goal. Avoiding contact of words or
eyes like icebergs or U-boats in the north Atlantic night.
Just before I made the turn, I noticed an assembly
of strange shapes and colors out of my peripheral.
My eyes move upward and become fixated on this
girl, maybe in her early-to-mid-twenties, and she was
wearing a wedding dress.

She stood in front of a tall mirror looking at the
ground, ignoring her reflection. Her glasses held up
by the sharp ridge of her nose. She wore the dress
over her clothes and draped her deep unbrushed
brown hair over her left shoulder. The gown is
an aesthetic risk even for irony's sake. I could tell
the white acrylic wasn't as bright as it once was.
Almost gray with age or dust as though I was
seeing it through a deep fog. The ribbons of fabric
exploded from her shoulders. The patterns on her
torso and waist seemed too complex to be able
to complement the poofs of manic lace. A woman,

who I assume was her ecstatic mother, circled the
girl in a frantic dance. Chirping compliments and
praise, trying her best to play the cards dealt and
make the best of circumstance's bad hand. The girl
remained in her stoic trance as the mother continued
her animated sincerity. Still refusing to look
at her reflection and join in her mother's optimistic
delusions. Maybe she was praying for a better
dress or perhaps a better life, I'm not for certain.

I do hope she is happy when her day comes. I hope
the sun smiles for her that day. I hope the birds sing
hallelujah. I hope the people in attendance bring you
mountains of gifts, I hope the cake is sweet, and I hope
that whoever she is marrying is just as happy as she is.

As much as I hope and pray
I know
Not every dog has its day
And not every bride gets a beautiful dress
But hoping doesn't hurt.
I didn't find a coat.
It's going to be a cold winter this year.

History Channel

8:30 AM
Didn't sleep
Maybe, 3-5 hours the night before
Former acquaintance bought a house
    a picture was posted as evidence for the purchase.
It got 50 likes
I just spilt White Castle honey mustard on my t-shirt
(Saved sauce packet / used on a bologna sandwich)
The TV is on
Caligula was a masochistic sexual deviant
It said from the other room
I get up to turn it off
And try to sleep again.

No applause for Nero
I guess.

The Gates of Hell Don't Have a Doorbell

Can't reason with the wind,
Nor can you ask the sky why.
Fate is a tangible forever;
Absurd is never and always
It's the rocking chair
The womb
The flower petals spread across the tomb.
I can hear Agent Smith crawling in my walls
Whispering,
Soon my child soon.

314 Fallujah

314 Fallujah,
Peace is an illusion.

Waters rising,
Drown in the grievance.

Gown made of soul,
Release us,
Make us whole.

Funeral homes and dealers,
Profit the same pocket.

Boy you leakin!
Foaming over crusty lips.

Gray days,
For a gray face,
Camouflage on the concrete.

The Pagedale Rambo is only 14,
But hey, at least your nails are clean.

She Came in Through the Bathroom Window

Exposed crocodile scars
Sewn deep into pink thighs,
Like shining medals of valor,
Whisper the horrors of war,
and victory over death.

Moving Day

Extended tape screech like car brakes
No time to fold up, decompress
Organize or file

Movement with disjointed purpose
Gravity becomes evident with each inching mile

Sit on the floor
   to catch my breath
Notice
   for the first time
   a stain on the ceiling tile

Every home
   has its stains.
Some hidden behind couches
   or under floorboards.

You could paint over them,
But you would have to
Drive to the mega size store,
   with its mega size parking
   lot, and its mega size customers.

Ask the worker with his mega size frown,
Hey, excuse me uh, where is the paint department?
Aisle 3? OK, thanks.

Did he have a lazy eye? It wasn't like totally cocked or
    anything, just like, so painfully,
    slightly,
    off on one side.
Each side is one side. Which side?
Fuck, what's stage left?
Right.
Right, that one.
I didn't see it.
Well it was.
And that's what makes it so off-putting
    you can't tell at first, but you know in your
    gut something is off.
Like when people don't have eyebrows?
Exactly.
Weird, well I didn't see it. OK, here it is, this is the color.

Buy the mega size paint
And the mega size brush
Wait in the mega size line
Buy a mega size Snickers

Turn on the radio for the drive home.
Can't think of anything new to listen to.
NPR is losing its touch.
Can't beat Fox News at being Fox News.
Try parallel parking in two different spaces before you
    give up and park down the block.

Can never get this door open.
Top lock,
right.
Bottom lock,
left.
Hard push.
The wooden frame with rusted mail slot swings open.
I am welcomed by the silhouette of my shadow on the other side of the room.
It sits right smack dab on top of the stain.
Shit better be worth the deposit.
Who am I kidding? Nobody gets their deposit back.

Icarus

Murder in August,
Upon a roof in mid-day.
Pushed beyond what the body can bear,
The mind is washed away like creek clay.
Look over the over row house skyline in absent state.
Cackling hyenas pester and bicker over a

    rotting carcass.
Dare Miguel to kill and hand him the electric blade,
Quite sure he lacks the will.
But to the surprise of the sweat-drenched crew,
Miguel's day was made.
Each ripple and tongue laps at the neck like
    reunited lovers.
The gutters do what they were made to do.
Wide eyes,
shock and awe,
Screams and laughter muzzled by the buzz
    of a circular saw.
If anything in this world is fair,
it's a dare,
because a dare is a dare.

Manifest Destiny

Jesus committed suicide by cop.
Gandhi was a pedophile.
Santa Claus has diabetes.
This city is falling apart because of eminent domain.
I can barely find the energy to do the dishes,
    let alone make a car bomb.
Don't say fuck it and post it on Facebook.
You'll ruin the surprise.

Existentialism Is for the Rich

A Medieval peasant, sometime in the middle ages, has
    an existential awakening whilst toiling in the fields.
He is digging a mud hole and stops abruptly.
His back straightens and his eyebrows furrow into the distance.
Past his hut made of sticks and human shit, and shit
    from various other medieval farm animals.

Why am I doing this?
Why must I toil and work for nothing?
    he asked the ducks as they waddled by.

You will be killed by the Lord of the castle,
    replied the pig, rubbing his belly in shit.

Oh, that's right.
    The peasant exclaimed, and promptly returned to his
    toiling and fruitless labor.

Ramen Noodle Zombies

When I was little
I lived on a little one-way
    street
In a little two-bedroom house
An ancient pine tree stood at attention over the
    sleepy brick huts
At night and clear as day
I would dream of flying down the stairs and
    out the window
I would dream of the sky falling in glorious
    splendor and fire
The bugs in the dirt lent good conversation
And I lent an ear to their sorrows
Even though the rollie pollies were shy, they
    were honest
Still mornings watching Pokémon with my
    dog and my cat
While everyone else was asleep
We enjoyed the peace
When the sun rose from the depths of space
Columns of zombies would wander out of
    the alley ways
And into the small houses
They would eat the flesh
And consume the soul

Twisting and ripping
Biting and chewing
There were no screams
Or cries for help
Death would take the day with the grace and poise of a
Victorian gentleman
I think everyone was just tired of fighting
Fighting for a little house on a little street
Fighting for bologna and Ramen noodles
Fighting for clean air
And let themselves become devoured
The current of blood swept through the street and
    down into the drains
The sun now was above us and stood watch
And dried the last of the blood

Leap of Faith

I used to think everything is pointless.
Now I think the apps on my phone are pointless.
To be honest,
I simply use them too much,
The problem was more likely excess.
Nietzsche wrote self-help books.
The Bible is a self-help book,
But with more death.
Buddhism is pacification in life,
Christianity is pacification in death,
Nihilism is animalistic in life and in death.

Elephant in the Tomb

I can't pretend another second
To be friends with the elephant
    in the room.

Knowing good and well
This mammoth wants me harmed
Shank me in the arm with its rusty tusks.

Any moment could be
A gust of anger,
A draft of danger from the open window.

I try to breathe slow
Anticipating pain turns the brain to anxiety mush.

Forget to flush
And watch the door shake.

More notes in the halls
Than gas station bathroom stalls.

I killed it for the ivory
    and now, I feel much better.

Bass Ackwards

First learned to walk on my fists
Before my feet;
It didn't look wrong in the mirror,
Until someone told me so.

Grew a backbone out my vocal chords;
I didn't know how loud I was,
    until someone told me so.

Pollinated all the flowers before the bees;
I didn't know how to love myself,
Until someone told me so.

Stole from Vicodin pack rats;
I didn't know it was funny,
Until someone told me so.

Wrestled with a bear at eye level;
Didn't know that wasn't funny,
Until someone told me so.

Modeled my behavior
    to that of a stale vanilla wafer;
I am exactly how I am today,
Because someone told me so.

Realm of Hungry Ghosts

Ayn Rand makes me moist.
Put me on the gurney.
Hoist and pull.
Grunt and struggle.
Squeaky wheels let 'em know I'm coming.
I'm hungry.
Time to eat something.
Foaming from my mouth hole,
Fill me.

Please
Dear god
Don't let me die.

I'm about to burst
With the holy spirit.
I don't stop when I'm full.
I stop when the food's gone the money's out

Gang way you ten-toed snakes
I'm coming home through the drive-thru.

The Black Hole

The baby's bare feet stand upon smoke-stained carpets.
She cries and cries as its diaper needs changing.
A lame dog sits in the corner waiting for scraps of fast food.
The air conditioner doesn't work
   and the stagnant air burns the skin,
   a rattling fan sits in front of the couch and
   battles the heat alone..
Feet march through the living room and out the door
   in a foreboding cadence.
The glass table is covered in filth,
   peppered in old food, unwashed dishes, scales,
   and baggies.
This black hole does not cater to race or age,
   to mothers or fathers.
It is the tranquil gate that the desperate seek and
   consume for a meager fee.
A part of me is still there,
Sitting on that couch,
Hiding from the world outside,
Waiting for the bombs to stop falling.

My Frankenstein

Duct tape
Holds this machine together
Cursing and squealing at sudden grinding halts
    clawing out of first gear and into second

Hissing and shaking

At the stoplight
Look out your window
And admire my metal Frankenstein
We live for another day.

I Don't Take Care of My Things

I don't take care of my things.

They sit and rust, collecting skins of dust,
As I try to fit square dreams inside circle
 circumstances.

Happenstance and fickle opportunity,
What blade can cut deeper than reflection's scrutiny?

Brooding seahorse posture perched upon
 sedated bedlam,
Drowning in fathoms of bright and bold
 aluminum designs.

Why must absent astral fathers remind you
 to be kind?

Why must you acclaim conquest and glory, when
 you yourself have never crossed the Rhine?

When the lights go out on Broadway
 it would behoove you to shine.

Even if I decide to move,
The mice in my home will stay,
So too does time remain.

The best of me was yesterday's lunch,

Leftovers sitting cold for months.
Growing colors and hues, bills past due.

Maybe perhaps tomorrow, I'll do better.
Begin anew, Become a trend setter,
Write those letters, surely then I will feel better.

Become light as feather, despite megalomaniacal
    weather.

Dawn waits outside my window
    to place its crown of light upon my rotten mind.

I open my eyes, and begin to remember,
Nothing is ever right no matter how hard I try.

I'll remain polite as I piss on my own parade.
Confess to myself in this nest I have made.

If you are not stupid or brave,
You best start learning how to pray.

The Beats

What's the difference between the beatniks and the kids of today?
Nothing—rich kids are still pretending to be poor.
Sure, you can write a line and definitely afford to do a few.
Walk on the sidewalk
And complain about the cops.
Drink cheap beer.
Pretend you don't have the insurance that would fix your blotchy skin that comes with alcohol abuse.
Commit a crime.
Parents pay the fine.
Get into a fight.
Spend a night in jail.
Walk out with your head held high.
Look at you now,
Against the world,
The empire
That your daddy stole and said he built.
Your dirty thrift store shoes look a lot like white guilt.
You rebel against a trust fund.
If I rebel
I become a bum,
I go to jail,
My teeth fall out,
I get addicted and can't afford the rehab.
Even if you never read Bukowski
We all know how to make a list.

5 AM

5 AM and
I am judging a stranger on Facebook.
Some guy who made
a stupid comment on
stupid click bait.
What the fuck is going on?

Giant Steps

Can't keep up with these giant steps
Passion of a partisan at the gallows
Get down low
Walk with fingers and toes
Return to the sky and back below the dirt
Lie with a smile
Slow down
Speed up
Make it up as you go
Daily matters
Of spilt milk and family dinners
Playful negligence
A sinful promise
It all seems wrong
My choices all seem wrong
Vertigo from existential arpeggios
He breathes on 2 and 4
Kills on 1-8
Once I find my place
There's nothing left but sustain and dispelled
    carbon dioxide
My heart can't even stay on time
Blasting contractions in all directions

In an attempt
    to escape the madness
    my time to shine
And pour some sugar on these black and white bones
Yet I

Still sound, feel, like I'm behind

Linoleum Dreams

I lie on this hospital bed staring at the swirling
    wood panel floor.

The charcoal tastes like charcoal.

My mother whimpers at my side.

Nurses fondle needles abed my florescent flesh
Their huddled judgements at my genetic misfortune
echo from the hall.

The awareness, that my life had been decided that
February morning, slithered into the room and rested
its crooked grin upon my lap.

My fate was sealed.
A bum I will be,
A loser for the ages.

So be it, I thought,
As I sipped the black muck from the white cup
    and gander'd at the graceful tide of linoleum dreams
    around my bed.

I Thought We Was Kin?

Please God
Won't you send me a friend?
Being alone
Is not how I wanted to spend forever.

My kin's
All become strangers.
My sins
Have put us all in danger.

I'll see you when I see you
He said as he closed the door.

I'll believe it when I see it
Was my reply.

Bar Stool Brag

You said
You were passionate
About sex

Weird flex
But OK.

Corner Store Mass

Broken bones
in smelly blankets,
in the sunlight
feeling patient.

Beer guts
and flower fragrance,
in your eyes
I'm always naked.

Wings spread
and so does laughter,
we fall like dead leaves
what does it matter?

Humble prayers
are never heard,
ramble fakers
lost in the word.

See true blue
in shattered stained glass,
cater truth
at corner store mass.

After days like this
sleep never sounded so good,
the pastor sings
and I begin to dream.

Blood on the Maple Leaf

I don't know when I will see you again so
We dive into the green and hide in between
    the patient trees.

Silent hostages chained to the eternal mother.

You lie in the pine needles and maple leaves.

The summer air still scratching at the back of my neck,
    and like the heavy fermenting regret that saddles
        upon old age,
It folds us into the dirt and into each other's arms.

We bend and mold,
Until you break.

The blood burning bright against the rotting
    hues of fall.

You clenched the dirt in your fists,
And sang silent harmonies with the trees that
    surrounded us.

We dusted off our knees and emerged from youth
    as we broke the tree line,
Never to return,

Holding dirty clammy hands.

Starry-Eyed Strays

I met a dog on the street the other day.
He had no leash and no master to lead the way,
    left home to look for god and since then he's become a
    stray.

He asked me if I've seen god lately.
I told him no, but you know the devil always
    answers his phone.

But, you're just a dog,
A stick and bone are all you need.
You shouldn't be concerned with heavenly thrones.
All that is nice, he replied, but
I would rather have a ball, a god, and a place
    to call home.
Although if you see the devil please tell him I said hello.

I met a boxer in a bar the other night.
Perched high on a bar stool after another long fight.
His mind twisted tightly in knots from regrets
    not soon forgot.
His heart beats louder than most but
    lost his love for the gloves after he read Jean Paul Sartre

He asked me if have seen god lately.

I told him no, but you know the Devil always
   answers his phone.

Don't lose hope just yet,
Just because God is dead.
The ink isn't dry, and the cast isn't set.
Why should I try?
   he replied
To bleed for the applause of starry-eyed strays.
My face filed and my mind ground to mush,
I'd rather feel safe in the pews of a dimly lit church.
But if you see the Devil be sure to tell him I said hello.

This morning I looked in the mirror,
Forlorn and drawn to distinct conclusion.
The silence grows and my ears begin to ring,
Not knowing it's really the telephone that sings.
I answered in a rush of hush,
It was the Devil,
He called to ask me if I had seen God lately.
I told him no but you know the Devil always answers
   his phone.

Silence

Give me an answer
He shouted
spearing spit and gripping his talons deep
into Death's collar.
Death returned with only silence
His grip loosened
Death had answered his question.

Country Mouse

Buried your bone
in the bed of a pickup truck.

Then reached for the sun
when you ran out of luck.

So, you left for the city
cuz you're afraid of being stuck.

Packed up the feathers
in a leather suitcase;
wait for better weather
and you might change your mind.

So you take flight that night,
leave this all behind.

Hey little country mouse,
from a little country house,
playing fiddle in the middle of the food stamp line.

Eating cold fries with five-dollar wine,
scraping lines and dimes,
from the crust in your eyes.

Daddy knew the Devil
but didn't know the menu.
Now you're serving up hot plates
like man watcha into?

The city ain't everything you hoped it'd be,
whiskey throttle train gone off the rails,
another country mouse lost on the trail.

Ultraviolet

You're so special
Flirty little diddy
Just like a vegetable
Head is empty

All this attention
You deserve it
Not to mention
You deserve it

Yesterday is useless
Toothless and stale

Covered in bruises
Blushing and pale

Old cum dried up
On your denim jacket
Can't go back to school
Couldn't hack it

Good thing you're popular
Always in the circle
Singing karaoke

Make your point
Before you go back on the meds

I'm not manic
I'm just running from the feds

Talk, talk, talk
Without a breath
Instead
Wait for them to stop
Grind and chew
Til your teeth crack
Tap, tap, tap
My toes might snap
Sweating bullets
Talk tacky like a mullet
I can't feel
Until Jesus pours down my gullet
Back to space
Up and down
Black out
Wake up in another town
Permanent frown
Smile while violent
Until
All
Becomes
Quiet

Whiskey Throttle

Can't make up my mind
Back and forth hiding from the thunder
If only I had more time to decide
Runaway train dripping trails of mascara
With swinging hoop ring dreams
All we needed was a mother
Now we exchange hangovers for apathetic lovers.

Toes in the water
Ripple green waves
Jesus only saves the babes with blue eyes before
They become spies
Fickle martyrs make good preachers

It's all downhill from here
This is the best it's ever gonna get
I always skip the prologue
I'd rather be surprised and confused
The plot ain't all that great
And the dialogue is butter-knife dull
What do I have to look forward to?
Now that I know the punchline
I'm sure it will be fine in due time
But until then I'll just pretend that I'm alright.

The Nest

Dirty laundry splayed across the floor
Heavy and
Hole ridden,
Lead filled,
Cotton cadavers.
Blessed is this mess
From between the window blinds,
White tape sunlight outlines my quiet crime scene.
Chest compressed until regular heart beats return
When will you learn?
To break bread and ribs from flower petals
Make lemonade from crimson puddles.

Blood rots in shy smiles from across the bar.
Let me be your maggot.
My life depends on your demise,
Your cooling dermis,
Your stagnant stare,
Your brilliant stillness.
Lips turn from red to blue like Alaskan sunsets,
Stale breath.
Shake my head for an hour.
My hands tremble.
My left eye twitches.
My heart swings.
It was you or me.

Dick Cheney Shot Someone and Got Away With It

Them Pashtun cowboys came flying around the bend;
Riding on their horses with AKs and Dracos in their hands;

Firing in all directions,
    the thunder in the canyon was tremendous.
The lonely mountain plateau had never seen this blood shed before.

Could it be repentance?
The holy bone soup we sought after?
The gods of the cowboy,
Tell em to die with a name.
But who would've thought
That their master was the same.

I Love Lamp

Your daddy was right in not liking me
He knew the truth
I was a loser
A bus riding bum

I rode
4 buses
2 trains
For 2 hours
Just to see you

But he knew the truth
I was going nowhere
Faster than my father shaved my head

I made you smile
And we talked for hours
About our shared love for Nina Simone

Hopping across the proverbial archipelago
Hand in hand
Deeper and deeper into the wide and blue singularity

But he knew the truth
I was too dumb
To make money
For you

Love doesn't pay the bills
Doesn't buy cheap thrills
Plane tickets
College funds
Or diapers

Sometimes I wonder
If you too
Saw your daddy's truth
Through those amber red colored lenses

But I knew as well as him
A boy with nothing
Would do anything
For you

Mackenzie Thorn is a poet from St. Louis, Missouri. Growing up he has lived in almost every corner, nook, and cranny of his home town. Worked a broad array of conventional and unconventional jobs like drug rehabilitation and dry wall hanging. He also spent 6 years in the Navy reserve. Published works in *Badjacket zine* and the *Rye Whiskey Review*.